Everyday
KINDNESS

It is a better feeling to give
than to receive you'll find.

And every day is a fresh chance
to show you can be kind.

Bake a special treat for someone in your neighborhood.

Treating someone kindly will make you both feel good.

Write a nice note on the sidewalk
for all who pass your way.

You'll bring a smile to their faces
and maybe even make their day.

Spread Love
every where you
go.

"the
best way
out is
through"

When it ☆ When it's ☆
rains, ☆ dark, look ☆
look ☆ for stars.
for ☆ ☆
rainbows.

Difficult
road often
lead to beautiful
destinations

If we weren't ourselves,
if we didn't make mistakes
we
wouldn't
be
us

BE
yourself

A new outfit or toy for
a child that is in need.

Donate to a school a book that
you no longer read.

Do a chore for mom and dad
before they even ask.

You'll feel all warm and fuzzy
when you're finished with your task.

Volunteer with your family
at a local food bank.

Help your brother or your sister
clean the family fish tank.

Complement a friend or
even someone you don't know.

Spend time with a grandparent,
let them teach you how to sew.

Say thank you to a teacher who does so much for you.

You can even write a note and draw a picture too.

Make a gift for someone
that you create special by hand.

Treat your neighbors to a free warm
up at your hot chocolate stand.

FREE Hot cocoa

Kindness is contagious,
so pass it on today.

Your kind words and actions
will soon come back your way.

Kind Acts to Try

- ☐ Bake a treat for a neighbor or friend
- ☐ Write a kind or inspirational note on the sidewalk
- ☐ Buy a new outfit for a child in need
- ☐ Donate a toy to a seasonal toy drive
- ☐ Do a chore for your parents
- ☐ Volunteer with your family at a local food bank
- ☐ Clean up your room without being asked
- ☐ Say Thank You!
- ☐ Compliment someone
- ☐ Host a free lemonade or hot chocolate stand
- ☐ Write a note or draw a picture for someone special
- ☐ Spend time with a grandparent
- ☐ Read to a younger child
- ☐ Make a gift by hand for a friend or family member
- ☐ Smile at everyone you see
- ☐ Collect loose change and donate it
- ☐ Help make dinner
- ☐ Make a bird feeder
- ☐ Write a letter to a military member
- ☐ Hold the door for someone
- ☐ Let someone go ahead of you in line
- ☐ Write a letter to a relative
- ☐ Invite someone new to play
- ☐ Make someone laugh
- ☐ Decorate and hide a kindness rock
- ☐ Give someone a flower
- ☐ Hide a few dollar bills around town
- ☐ Plant a tree

www.ingramcontent.com/pod-product-compliance
Lightning Source LLC
Chambersburg PA
CBHW040316100426
42811CB00012B/1462

* 9 7 8 0 5 7 8 4 1 1 5 8 3 *